BEER

MAKES DADDY STRONG

HODDER &
STOUGHTON

ANDY RILEY IS THE AUTHOR/ARTIST OF THE BOOK OF BUNNY SUICIDES, DAWN OF THE BUNNY SUICIDES AND EVERY OTHER BUNNY SUICIDE THING. HIS OTHER BOOKS INCLUDE GREAT LIES TO TELL SMALL KIDS, LOADS MORE LIES TO TELL SMALL KIDS, SELFISH PIGS, ROASTED AND D.I.Y. DENTISTRY.

HIS SCRIPTWRITING WORK INCLUDES BLACK BOOKS, THE GREAT OUTDOORS, HYPERDRIVE, LITTLE BRITAIN, ARMSTRONG AND MILLER, GNOMEO & JULIET, THE ARMANDO IANNUCCI SHOWS, HARRY+PAUL, SLACKER CATS AND THE BAFTA-WINNING ANIMATION ROBBIE THE REINDEER.

misterandyriley.com

FIRST PUBLISHED IN GREAT BRITAIN IN 2010 BY
HODDER AND STOUGHTON, AN HACHETTE UK COMPANY

COPYRIGHT © 2011 BY ANDY RILEY

3

HARDBACK ISBN 978 1 444 71104 2

PRINTED & BOUND IN ITALY BY L.E.G.O. SPA

HODDER & STOUGHTON POLICY IS TO USE PAPERS MADE
FROM WOOD GROWN IN SUSTAINABLE FORESTS.
THE LOGGING & MANUFACTURING PROCESSES ARE
EXPECTED TO CONFORM TO THE ENVIRONMENTAL
REGULATIONS OF THE COUNTRY OF ORIGIN.

HODDER AND STOUGHTON 338 EUSTON ROAD,
LONDON NW1 3BH
WWW.HODDER.CO.UK

WITH THANKS TO:
GORDON WISE, LISA HIGHTON
AND ALL AT HODDER, POLLY
FABER AND KEVIN CECIL.

MAN
FLU

DADDY WOULD RATHER
YOU DIDN'T LAUGH
AT IT

CHIPS

ARE WHAT DAD
STEALS OFF YOUR
PLATE WHEN HE
SAID HE DIDN'T
WANT ANY

"WHO'S THE DADDY?"

IS WHAT DADDY
LIKES TO SAY SOMETIMES

IT'S PROBABLY FROM
A FILM OR SOMETHING

IT MAKES HIM HAPPY, ANYWAY

THE INTERESTING ARTICLE <u>NEXT</u> TO THE BREASTS

<u>THAT'S</u> WHAT DADDY'S LOOKING AT

CONVERSATIONS WITH DAD

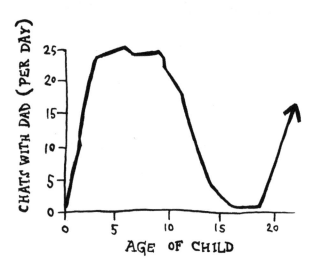

THEY WILL RETURN,
IN THE END

WAR FILMS

MAKE DADDY
FEEL BRAVE
IN HIS HEAD

KITE

IF YOU CAN'T
GET IT IN THE
AIR YOU WON'T FEEL
LIKE A PROPER DAD

A NEW PHONE

DADDY REALLY
REALLY WANTS ONE

ABOUT 2 WEEKS AFTER
HE GOT THE LAST ONE

THE 'FLOORDROBE'

DADDY SAYS HE
PIONEERED THE CONCEPT

THOSE COLOURFUL TIES

THAT YOU BOUGHT FOR
DADDY ON PREVIOUS FATHERS'
DAYS ARE KEPT IN A
SPECIAL DRAWER

SO SPECIAL IN FACT

THAT THEY NEVER
COME OUT
OF IT

TOY STORY 3

IT WAS NICE AND
DARK IN THE CINEMA

SO NO-ONE SAW
DADDY CRY

SPAGHETTI BOLOGNESE

DAD COOKS A GREAT ONE

GOOD JOB TOO CAUSE IT'S ABOUT
THE ONLY THING HE CAN COOK

SO IF YOU DON'T
LIKE IT – TOUGH

TREE
HOUSES

OF *COURSE*
DADDY KNOWS HOW
TO BUILD ONE

AIRFIX KITS

MAKE DADDY NOSTALGIC
WHEN HE SEES THEM
IN SHOPS

BUT HE DOESN'T ACTUALLY
WANT TO BUILD ONE ANY
TIME SOON SO DON'T
BUY HIM ONE
FOR HIS BIRTHDAY

DIVING BOARDS

FEAR

CALM EXTERIOR

ADMIRATION

A DAD ALWAYS HAS TO PROVE HE CAN JUMP OFF THE HIGHEST ONE

THE BOUNCY CASTLE

DADDY LIKES A GO ON IT AT THE END OF THE KIDS' PARTY

ALONG WITH THE OTHER DADDIES

STITCHES

DADDY GOT THREE
OF THEM AFTER HE
BOUNCED OUT OF
THE BOUNCY CASTLE

HE DOESN'T LIKE TO
TALK ABOUT IT

THE CAMPING HOLIDAY

WAS DEFINITELY
DADDY'S IDEA

THAT'S WHAT MUMMY
KEEPS SAYING ANYWAY

AN INCURABLE ROMANTIC

.... SOMETIMES DADDY REMEMBERS TO BE ONE (ONCE EVERY COUPLE OF YEARS)

VINDALOO CURRIES

DADDY'S GOT TO PRETEND
HE ENJOYS THEM

IT'S PART OF BEING A MAN

MID-LIFE CRISIS CARS

DADDY KNOWS
THEY'RE STUPID

BUT HE WANTS
ONE ANYWAY

DADDY'S OLD VINYL

SOMEHOW

DADDY CAN'T BRING
HIMSELF TO THROW IT AWAY

SCARS

DAD LOVES
TO SHOW
THEM OFF

(*LIE)

MAP-READING

A PRIME
"DADDY SKILL"

NOW MADE IRRELEVANT
BY SATNAV TECHNOLOGY

THE DVD OF MAMMA MIA

OTHERWISE KNOWN AS 'DADDY KRYPTONITE'

"THE MOVES

DADDY'S STILL GOT THEM
THEY MOSTLY COME
OUT AT WEDDINGS

TRIUMPH

THE FEELING DADDY GETS WHEN
HE FINDS A MEMORY STICK
CONTAINING THE FIRST TWO YEARS
OF CHILD PHOTOS, THOUGHT LOST
WHEN THE COMPUTER DIED

MIXED IN WITH A BIT OF RELIEF

CAUSE MUMMY WON'T KILL HIM NOW

WALKING THE DOG

ALWAYS SEEMS TO
BE DADDY'S JOB
WHEN IT'S RAINING

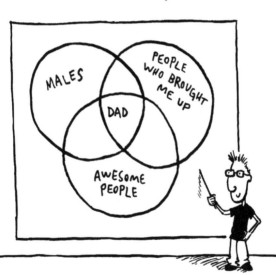

VENN DIAGRAMS

MALES

PEOPLE WHO BROUGHT ME UP

DAD

AWESOME PEOPLE

...MAKE EVERYTHING CLEAR

HITLER DOCUMENTARIES

DAD CAN WATCH THREE IN A ROW

GOING TO THE TIP

DADDY PRETENDS IT'S A CHORE
BUT REALLY IT'S ONE OF
HIS FAVOURITE THINGS

SHOPPING

IS NOT SOMETHING DADDY REGARDS AS A LEISURE ACTIVITY IN ITS OWN RIGHT

DAD'S TAXI CO.

- 24 HOURS A DAY
- 365 DAYS A YEAR

SUNDAY PAPERS

GIVE DAD A
GREAT PLACE
TO HIDE

THE Wii

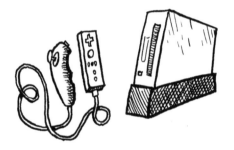

DADDY BOUGHT IT
'FOR THE KIDS'

YEAH, RIGHT

PORK
SCRATCHINGS

TWO PINTS IN,
AND DADDY CAN'T
RESIST THEM

POWERPOINT

DAD MIGHT START
USING IT AT HOME
AS WELL AS WORK

GARDENING:

- MUMMY PLANTS STUFF
- DADDY CHOPS IT BACK

PARENTS' EVENINGS

DAD ALWAYS PUTS
IN THE RESEARCH

£800
FOR A HANDBAG

DADDY WILL NEVER UNDERSTAND *THAT*

SHOULDER RIDES

ALWAYS WERE A
MAGICAL MOMENT
WITH
DAD

GOALKEEPERS

ONE DAY, DADDY NOTICED THEY
WERE THE ONLY PROFESSIONAL
FOOTBALLERS THE SAME AGE AS HIM

EVEN THEN

ONLY THE OLD GOALKEEPERS

SuRViViNG IN THE WiLD

DADDY KNOWS HE'D BE VERY GOOD AT IT BECAUSE HE'S WATCHED A *LOT* OF TELLY ABOUT IT

AT THE DENTIST

THE ONLY TIME
DADDY SHOWS FEAR

GRAND CHILDREN

MAKE DADDY PROUD ALL OVER AGAIN

THE
WEDDING
ANNIVERSARY

ONE DAY, SOMEONE WILL EXPLAIN
TO DADDY WHY IT'S ALWAYS THE
MAN'S JOB TO REMEMBER IT

AND

AND !!

REFILL REQUIRED